W9-CFV-317

Solar Power

by Richard Hantula

Science and Curriculum Consultant:
Debra Voege, M.A.,
Science Curriculum Resource Teacher

CHELSEA CLUBHOUSE
An Imprint of Chelsea House Publishers

Energy Today: Solar Power

Chelsea Clubhouse
An imprint of Chelsea House Publishers
132 West 31st Street
New York NY 10001

Library of Congress Cataloging-in-Publication Data
Hantula, Richard.
        Solar power / by Richard Hantula; science and curriculum consultant, Debra Voege.
             p. cm. — (Energy today)
        Includes index.
        ISBN 978-1-60413-779-8
         1. Solar energy—Juvenile literature. I. Title.
    TJ810.3.H365 2010
    333.792'3—dc22   2009036864

Chelsea Clubhouse books are available at special discounts when purchased in bulk quantities for businesses, associations, institutions, or sales promotions. Please call our Special Sales Department in New York at (212) 967-8800 or (800) 322-8755.

You can find Chelsea Clubhouse on the World Wide Web at http://www.chelseahouse.com

Developed for Chelsea House by RJF Publishing LLC (www.RJFpublishing.com)
Project Editor: Jacqueline Laks Gorman
Text and cover design by Tammy West/Westgraphix LLC
Illustrations by Spectrum Creative Inc.
Photo research by Edward A. Thomas
Index by Nila Glikin
Composition by Westgraphix LLC
Cover printed by Bang Printing, Brainerd, MN
Book printed and bound by Bang Printing, Brainerd, MN
Date printed: May 2010
Printed in the United States of America

Photo Credits: 5: iStockphoto; 6: © Stock Connection Blue/Alamy; 10: DOE/NREL; 12: NASA; 15: Randy Montoya and Sandia National Laboratories; 17: Juan Carlos Munoz/age fotostock/Photolibrary; 18: U.S. Air Force photo/Airman 1st Class Nadine Y. Barclay/NREL; 21: Brand X Pictures/age fotostock; 25: DOE/NREL; 26: DOE/NREL; 27: Getty Images; 29: iStockphoto; 31: Carlos S. Pereyra/age fotostock/Photolibrary; 32: Ian Williams, Channel Islands National Park; 35: NASA; 38: AP Images; 39: NASA; 40: DOE/NREL; 42: AP Images; 43: ROGER L. WOLLENBERG/UPI/Landov.

10 9 8 7 6 5 4 3 2 1

This book is printed on acid-free paper.

All links and Web addresses were checked and verified to be correct at the time of publication. Because of the dynamic nature of the Web, some addresses and links may have changed since publication and may no longer be valid.

TABLE OF CONTENTS

Words that are defined in the Glossary are in **bold**
type the first time they appear in the text.

CHAPTER 1

Energy and the Sun

Energy makes things happen. It makes cars go and makes machines run. When you feel warm, you are feeling heat energy. When you see things, it is thanks to the energy called light.

The Sun is the biggest source of energy in our lives. The Sun gives off enormous amounts of heat and light in all directions. It has shone for billions of years. Scientists say it will continue to shine for billions of years in the future.

Earth is located very far from the Sun—about 93 million miles (150 million kilometers) away. This means that Earth gets only a small part of the energy that the Sun puts out. That energy output is so big, however, that a huge amount of light and heat reaches Earth. We call this energy solar energy, which means that it is from the Sun.

This solar energy drives the winds. It also powers the currents in the ocean (the movement of ocean waters). In fact, solar energy makes life on Earth possible. Life depends on water, and heat from the Sun causes a process called the water cycle. In this cycle, water constantly moves between Earth's surface and the air, or atmosphere, above it. The Sun's heat causes water to evaporate into the air. Eventually, this water falls back to the ground as rain or snow.

Solar energy makes life possible in another important way as well. Sunlight gives plants the energy they need to make

The Sun is the biggest source of energy in our lives.

food in a process called photosynthesis. During photosynthesis, plants take in sunlight, use water, and put oxygen into the air.

Using Solar Energy in Daily Life

The Sun's heat and light have many uses. To help plants grow, some people build greenhouses, which collect solar heat. Some people rely on the Sun to dry their clothes after washing. Some people boil water or cook food using the heat of the Sun's rays.

Sunlight is also used to produce one of our most important forms of energy: electricity. There are a couple of different methods to do this. Each method can be used in power stations, or **power plants**. These are large facilities that supply electricity to the public power system, which is also known as the **grid**.

Each method of producing electricity can also be used in smaller power-supply systems. Such smaller systems can meet

Greenhouses collect the Sun's heat. They are used to help plants grow.

some or all of the electricity needs of a machine, a small house, or another kind of building. The systems can be used by people who do not want to rely on the grid. They can also be used in places where the grid is so far away that connecting to it would cost too much or would be impossible. In addition, the systems can come in handy when it is simply not convenient to connect to the grid.

One of the methods of using sunlight to produce electricity uses the Sun's heat to run a machine that generates electricity. The other method of using sunlight is particularly **versatile**. It relies on small **devices** called **solar cells**. Solar cells make electricity directly from sunlight. These cells are good power sources for small things like outdoor lights, highway signs, and water pumps on farms. They are often used to power small electronic devices such as calculators.

Groups of solar cells—which are called **solar arrays**—are used where larger amounts of power are needed. Solar arrays are sometimes used to make electricity in large power stations. Solar arrays (and sometimes smaller numbers of solar cells) can be a good source of electricity for remote villages that are located far from any grid. Solar arrays are also a common power source on spacecraft and space stations.

Top Fuels

Most of the energy people use today comes from fuels like coal, oil, and natural gas. These are examples of **fossil fuels**. For a long time, burning fossil fuels has been a common way to keep buildings warm. Fossil fuels are also used to power vehicles. Imagine how much gasoline and diesel fuel is used every year!

Did You Know?
Energy and Power

When people say "solar power," they usually mean electricity made from solar energy. Scientists, however, tend to use the words *energy* and *power* to mean certain specific things. For them, **power** is the rate at which work is done. It is measured in units such as **watts** and **megawatts** (one million watts). In contrast, energy is the ability to do work. It is measured in units such as kilowatt-hours and British thermal units (BTUs). One BTU is the amount of heat needed to raise the temperature of a pound (0.45 kilograms) of water by 1° Fahrenheit (0.56° Celsius).

Did You Know?

Making Electricity

To produce electricity, most power plants burn fossil fuels to boil water. When the water boils, it produces steam. The steam is then heated further so that it has enough pressure to turn the blades on a turbine. The hot steam pushes against the blades, causing the turbine to spin. The turbine is attached to one end of a long pole, or rod. The other end of the rod is connected to a generator. There are large magnets and metal coils inside the generator. When the rod turns, the magnets spin, producing electricity inside the coils. The electric current that is produced then makes its way along transmission lines to homes, office buildings, and wherever it is needed.

Gasoline and diesel fuel are the most popular fuels for cars, buses, and trucks. Both are made from oil—which makes them fossil fuels.

Fossil fuels are also the most common energy source for producing electricity. They are burned to make heat, which is used to make water boil and turn into steam. The steam runs a machine called a **turbine** that produces a turning action, which causes a **generator** to produce electricity.

Nuclear power is another key energy source today, providing about 6 percent of the world's energy. Nuclear power is an important way of generating electricity in countries such as France and the United States. It is also used to power certain kinds of ships.

Fossil fuels have many advantages. Currently, they are abundant—there is enough coal, oil, and natural gas to meet the world's needs. They work well, are easy to use, and are cheap enough for general use. They also have serious drawbacks, however. For one thing, they will not last forever. Earth has only a limited supply of fossil fuels, and once they are used, they are gone forever. In other words, they are not **renewable**. Another problem is that burning fossil fuels puts gases and other substances into the air that make the air dirty, or polluted. Scientists say that some of the gases may even change Earth's **climate**. Land and water may also be polluted by gases and dust from burning fossil fuels. They may be harmed as well by accidents involving fossil fuels, such as oil spills.

Nuclear power has some advantages. It does not cause the pollution that fossil fuels do. Also, there will probably be plenty of fuel for nuclear power plants in the future. Uranium is the main fuel currently used in nuclear plants. Earth's supply of uranium may run low at some point in the future, but other types of fuel for use in nuclear plants can be made easily.

Like fossil fuels, nuclear power has serious drawbacks. The chief one is that materials like uranium give off harmful **radiation**—radioactivity—that can cause sickness or death.

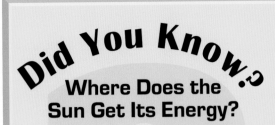

Did You Know?

Where Does the Sun Get Its Energy?

The Sun's energy comes from nuclear **fusion**. This process is quite different from the one used to produce nuclear power on Earth. Nuclear power plants use a process called fission. In fission, heavy atoms are split apart, creating smaller atoms plus radioactivity and energy—what we call nuclear energy. In fusion, light atoms—such as hydrogen—combine, or fuse. This process creates new, heavier atoms. It also releases a great deal of energy.

These students are collecting solar thermal energy to cook eggs.

Today's nuclear power plants have safeguards to keep radiation from leaking out. A serious accident or a **terrorist** attack, however, might still release dangerous radiation. Another problem is finding ways to dispose of **radioactive waste**. A permanent storage place has not yet been built for the most dangerous waste.

Alternative Fuels

Because of the drawbacks of fossil fuels and nuclear power, people have been looking for alternatives. The ideal source of energy would be cheap, abundant, and clean. It would also be renewable. Several alternative energy sources are in use today. Each has strong points and weak points.

Water power is an important energy source in some parts of the world. The force of falling water is used to drive turbines to generate electricity. Usually, dams are built for this purpose.

Water power is a renewable source. Dams, however, can be built only where there is a suitable stream of water. Also, dams and the **reservoirs** they create can damage the environment. Dams can stop fish from traveling upstream to produce their eggs. In addition, when a reservoir forms, it floods the land. This can destroy plants and kill or push out wildlife that lived in the area.

Wind, like water, is a renewable energy source. It is clean and found around the world. Some areas have less wind than others, though, and there is practically no place where the wind is always blowing. Because of this, wind cannot serve as a continuous supply of power.

Tidal power and geothermal energy are two alternative energies that are less commonly used. Tidal power relies on the movement of the **tides** to generate electricity. Suitable tides, however, occur only in certain parts of the world. Geothermal power relies on underground heat. It, too, can be used only in certain areas.

Did You Know?
The Sun Does It All

The Sun is responsible for most forms of energy used in the world today. Fossil fuels were formed from the remains of living things, which needed the Sun in order to live and grow. Wood—another common energy source—comes from trees, whose existence depends on sunlight. Modern **biofuels** are commonly made from crops like corn, sugarcane, or switchgrass, which also depend on the Sun. Wind power, water power, and tidal power are all a result of processes driven by the Sun.

Biofuels—fuels made from materials coming from plants or animals—are yet another alternative. Ethanol made from plants is an example. Since new plants can always be grown, biofuels are renewable. Biofuels, however, must be burned in order to produce energy. This releases gases into the air that may be harmful. Another drawback is

In Their Own Words

"We...should be using Nature's inexhaustible sources of energy—sun, wind and tide. I'd put my money on the sun and solar energy. What a source of power! I hope we don't have to wait until oil and coal run out before we tackle that."

Inventor Thomas Edison, 1931

The International Space Station has giant solar arrays that provide power.

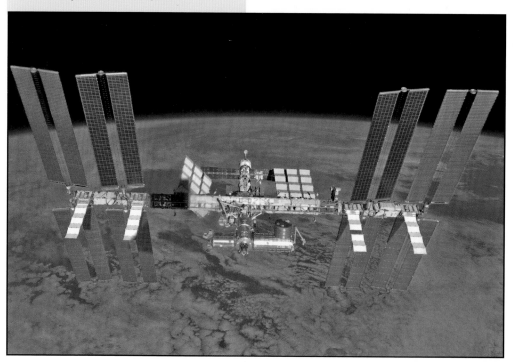

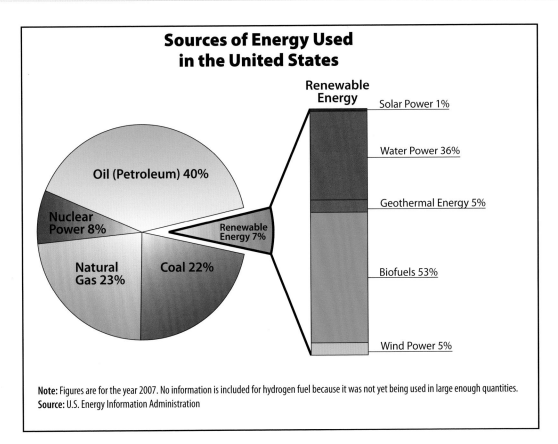

Sources of Energy Used in the United States

Oil (Petroleum) 40%

Nuclear Power 8%

Natural Gas 23%

Coal 22%

Renewable Energy 7%

Renewable Energy

Solar Power 1%

Water Power 36%

Geothermal Energy 5%

Biofuels 53%

Wind Power 5%

Note: Figures are for the year 2007. No information is included for hydrogen fuel because it was not yet being used in large enough quantities.
Source: U.S. Energy Information Administration

that growing the plants uses a lot of land. That land cannot be used for other purposes, such as growing food crops.

That leaves solar energy. Solar energy is extremely abundant and almost completely renewable: The Sun's power will last almost forever. Currently, however, solar energy makes up only a tiny portion of the energy used in the United States. In 2007, renewable energy made up just 7 percent of U.S. energy consumption. Solar energy accounted for only 1 percent of that renewable energy. In the foreseeable future, solar energy may not produce major amounts of the world's power supply. Nevertheless, as the use of solar energy grows in the United States and the world, solar energy may well play an important role in the world's energy future.

Putting Solar Energy to Work

CHAPTER 2

There are many ways solar energy can be put to work. Some are known as **active methods**. Others are called **passive methods**. An active method for putting solar energy to work makes use of electrical or mechanical equipment—for example, a pump. Passive methods use little or no electrical or mechanical help. A greenhouse is an example of a passive method, since it collects the Sun's heat without any type of equipment.

There are also two basic ways to make electricity from solar energy. One uses solar cells, which convert sunlight directly into electricity. This approach is called **photovoltaic**. (*Photo* means "light," and *voltaic* refers to electricity.) Solar cells are often called photovoltaic cells, or **PV** cells, for short. The other approach to making electricity is called thermal. (*Thermal* comes from a Greek word meaning "heat.") Solar thermal power systems use the Sun's heat to run a machine that generates electricity.

Active and Passive Solar Power

The words *active* and *passive* are used mostly when talking about the use of solar energy for such purposes as heating, cooling, or ventilation. A solar-energy system that uses a machine like a fan to move air is active. A passive system, in contrast, does its job using only the help of nature. For instance,

The SunCatcher has a large mirror that collects and concentrates heat, which drives a device called a Stirling engine. The engine produces a turning movement, which runs a generator, producing electricity.

heated air is lighter than cool air and naturally tends to rise. A passive system might make use of this fact.

A greenhouse uses a different passive method. A greenhouse is designed for warmth. It has a clear glass or plastic roof that lets sunshine in. At the same time, the roof keeps warm air from getting out. Another structure using passive solar power is a house with many windows that face south. It relies on the fact that south-facing windows get the most sunshine. (Of course, this is true only for buildings in the United States, Canada, and other areas in the northern half of the world. In the southern half, the home's windows would need to face north!)

Solar Heating and Cooking

Some buildings and swimming pools use Sun-heated water. A typical solar water-heating system has two main parts. One is a collector, where water is heated. The other is a tank, where the heated water is held. (With a swimming pool, the pool itself serves as the tank.) Tubes link the two parts. A common type of

collector—known as a flat-plate collector—looks like a flat box. This collector might be put on a roof. The box's cover is transparent, so sunlight can pass through it. A liquid, such as water, flows through small tubes in the box. The water gets heated by sunlight and goes to the tank.

Such a system may be passive or active. A passive system uses nature to move the water. It might rely on the downward force of gravity and on heated water's tendency to move. An active system might use a pump. It might also have a device that moves the collector to keep the collector pointed at the Sun. The Sun moves across the sky during the course of a day. By "tracking" the Sun, the collector gets as much sunlight as possible.

There also are cookers and furnaces that use the Sun's heat. They usually have a large surface that is a mirror or is made of shiny metal. This surface has a special shape, making it look like a box or a dish. When the Sun's rays fall on the surface, its shape and shininess make the rays bounce, or be reflected, so that they join together. A small device of this sort can make enough heat to cook food. Small solar cookers or ovens can be lifesavers in areas of the world where there is not enough wood or other fuel.

The solar furnace at Odeillo, France, has 63 mirrors to catch sunlight.

Large solar furnaces can produce high heat. They can be used for research or manufacturing. A solar furnace at Odeillo, France—which is used for research—has 63 flat mirrors to catch sunlight. These mirrors have a total area of about 30,515 square feet (2,835 square meters). They serve as "**concentrators**," collecting as much sunlight as possible for the furnace. They reflect the sunlight onto a giant curved mirror that is 130 feet (40 meters) tall. The curved mirror focuses all the sunlight into a small area. In this area, the temperature can rise to as high as 5400°F (3000°C).

Making Electricity with Solar Cells

A solar, or PV, cell is like a computer chip. Both are made of materials known as **semiconductors**. They are called that because they can carry, or conduct, electricity. The *semi* is tacked on because they do not conduct electricity as well as metals do. The semiconductor used in a solar cell does something very interesting. It can absorb light of a certain wavelength, or color. When sunlight falls on the cell, some of it gets reflected. Some may get turned into heat, and some might pass right through the cell. Light with the right wavelength, however, may get absorbed. The semiconductor material then gives off a bit of electricity. In this way, a solar cell can be used to produce an electric current.

Various semiconductor materials are used to make solar cells. Silicon is the most common. Cells also come in different sizes. The smallest are tinier than a postage stamp, while large ones can be several inches across or more. For some purposes, such as a small battery charger, one solar cell might be enough. If more electricity is needed, several cells can be joined together. This grouping is called a **solar module**, or **solar panel**. If still more power is needed, several modules can be joined together in a solar array. A large PV power station may use thousands of panels.

Some solar panels have special systems to help them get as much sunlight as possible. For instance, a tracking system may keep the panels facing the Sun as it moves through the sky. Concentrators may also be used for this purpose. These are

Thousands of solar panels are lined up at Nellis Air Force Base in Nevada. The base has one of the largest PV power plants in the United States.

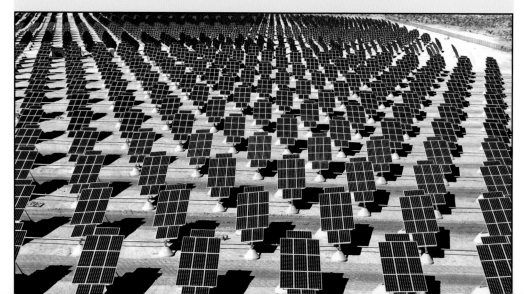

CLARENCE KEMP

Clarence Kemp, an inventor and businessman from Baltimore, Maryland, is known as the father of solar energy in the United States. Kemp used his creativity to solve a common problem in the late nineteenth century—how hard it was to heat large amounts of water. People could heat water in a pan on the stove top, but sometimes they wanted more than that amount, so they filled large metal tanks with water and placed them in the sunlight. After many hours, the water got hot. As soon as the Sun went down, though, the water cooled off. Kemp came up with a system, using a network of black-painted pipes in an insulated box, that kept the water hot for a much longer time. He called his invention the Climax. Kemp **patented** his invention—the first commercial solar water heater—in 1891.

devices such as lenses or mirrors that can direct more sunshine to the cells.

In 2008, Nellis Air Force Base in Nevada had the largest PV power plant in the United States. It uses almost 6 million solar cells. They make up more than 72,000 solar panels, which can track the Sun. The whole array covers 140 acres (57 hectares) of land. It can generate up to 14 megawatts of electric power and supplies about a fourth of the base's electricity. An even larger PV plant, called the DeSoto Next Generation Solar Energy Center, was being built in Florida in 2009. It will cover 180 acres (73 hectares) of land and generate 25 megawatts of electricity—which is enough to meet the needs of thousands of homes and people. There are also large PV power plants in Europe and South Korea. The Olmedilla Photovoltaic Park in Spain, for example, can generate up to 60 megawatts of electricity.

Plans for other large PV plants are in the works, but PV power stations cannot yet produce as much power as other types of power plants. For example, today's biggest fossil-fuel or nuclear

RUSSELL OHL

In 1839, French scientist Edmond Becquerel discovered that light can make materials give off electricity. Solar cells came along much later. The first solar cell more or less like today's solar cells was invented by U.S. engineer Russell Ohl, who was born in 1898 in Pennsylvania. Ohl was only 16 years old when he went to college at Pennsylvania State University. During college, he developed a strong interest in radio tubes. Ohl got a job at Bell Laboratories in New Jersey in 1927. At Bell Labs, while trying to develop better radio tuners, he did important research on semiconductors. As part of this work, he developed his solar cell. He filed for a patent on it in 1941. He called his cell a "light-sensitive electric device." Like many modern solar cells, it was made of silicon. Bell Labs developed the first practical solar cell in 1954. It made enough electricity to run ordinary electrical devices. Ohl's research also helped prepare the way for a later important development: the invention of the **transistor**. Ohl died in 1987.

plants may have a capacity of 1,000 megawatts or more. PV power stations have a long way to go before they can compare with these types of plants.

In recent years, a new type of solar cell—called a thin-film cell—has come into use. Such cells are made of extremely thin layers. The layers are thinner than four ten-thousandths of an inch (a thousandth of a centimeter). Thin-film solar cells can cover a large area. They can be put on surfaces like roof tiles, building walls, and skylights. They also can be used for personal electronic devices and battery chargers.

Solar Thermal Power

Solar thermal power systems collect heat energy from sunshine. They then convert the heat energy into a turning movement.

Then, a generator converts the turning movement into electric current.

Solar thermal power systems need high temperatures to work. They can collect the Sun's heat in different ways. Usually, they use some form of concentrator to get as much heat as possible. One common method uses a long, specially shaped trough. It looks something like a gutter that collects rainwater at the edge of a roof, but it is larger and has a curved surface. A tube carrying a liquid, such as oil, runs along the inside of the trough. The surface of the trough is a mirror. Sunshine that hits it is reflected to the tube, which heats the liquid inside the tube. The hot liquid then flows to another part of the system. There, its heat is used to boil water to make steam. This steam

A solar power tower—such as this one, in California—produces electricity using many mirrors that direct sunlight to the top of the tower.

How a Solar Power Tower Works

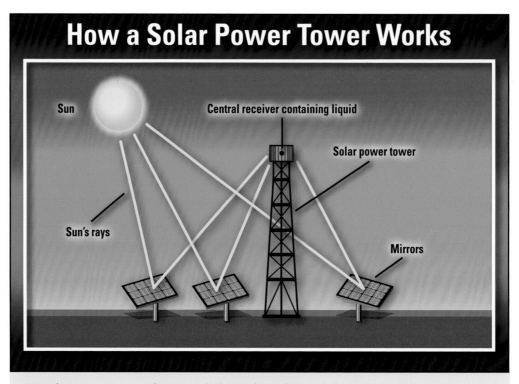

Sun

Central receiver containing liquid

Solar power tower

Sun's rays

Mirrors

In a solar power tower, mirrors track the Sun's motion and direct the sunlight to the top of the tower. There, a liquid is heated and used to create steam for a turbine, which runs a generator.

drives a turbine, creating a turning movement that a generator converts into electricity. (Sometimes the liquid heated in the trough is water. In this case, the water, heated to form steam, may drive the turbine directly.) One of the largest solar plants to use this technology is the Nevada Solar One power plant at Boulder City, Nevada, which was finished in 2007. The plant has 760 troughs, covers more than 400 acres (162 hectares), and can produce 64 megawatts of power—enough to power more than 14,000 homes.

Another major thermal method uses a large dish-shaped mirror. Sunshine that hits the mirror is reflected to one point. There, the light concentrates, resulting in high heat. This heat drives a device called a Stirling engine. The Stirling engine produces a turning movement, which runs a generator. A notable example is the SunCatcher, produced by Stirling Energy Systems. The SunCatcher's dish is 38 feet (11.6 meters) wide. As of 2009, the company was planning to build two solar power plants in California with thousands of dishes. Each SunCatcher dish would have its own Stirling engine. If fully built, the two plants would have a total capacity of 1,750 megawatts. There also are dish systems that do not use a Stirling engine. Instead, they use a steam turbine to run the generator.

Power Towers and Melted Salt

A third important thermal method uses a tall "power tower." Below the tower, many flat mirrors track the Sun's motion. The mirrors direct the sunlight they receive to the top of the tower. There, the sunlight heats a liquid. The hot liquid is used to create steam for a turbine, which runs a generator. The PS20 solar power plant near Seville, Spain, has a power tower. The tower is 531 feet (162 meters) tall. The plant, which opened in 2009, has a capacity of 20 megawatts. The sunshine used to make this electricity is collected by 1,255 mirrors. Each mirror has an area of 1,291 square feet (120 square meters).

Solar thermal power systems typically include some means of storing heat. They can use this heat to produce electricity even when the Sun is not shining. A common way to store heat is to have one or more tanks of very hot liquid. Often, this hot liquid is molten salt—salt that has been heated so that it turns into a thick liquid. When salt is melted in this way, it can hold a great deal of heat. There is enough heat to run generators to produce electricity for hours.

CHAPTER 3

Big Benefits

It is easy to see why many people like the idea of using solar energy. For one thing, sunlight is free. Nobody has to pay the Sun for the energy it supplies. Moreover, the supply of sunlight is always there. The Sun never turns off. It has shined for billions of years and is expected to keep on shining for billions of years to come.

Solar energy has another big advantage: There is a great deal of it. According to one estimate, the amount of energy Earth receives from the Sun in just one hour is almost as great as the total amount of energy all the people of the world consume in a year. Also, as we have seen, solar energy can be used in many different ways.

Power Points

Making electricity is one of the most important uses of solar energy, and solar power has a number of strong points. Small solar thermal or PV power systems can come in handy when it is not possible to have a link to the grid. They also can be a good alternative when a link to the grid may be inconvenient or very costly.

For things that need only a little power, like signs, solar cells or panels can be just what is needed. They are easy to transport. They also do not break down, which is why they are often used to power things like highway signs, outdoor

Solar power can be used to run water pumps on farms.

telephones, water pumps on farms, and lights in remote villages. The U.S. Army even has tents with thin-film solar cells. These can provide power for phones, laptop computers, and other equipment.

Solar power can also be helpful in homes or other buildings that are linked to the grid. Since the fuel used—sunshine—is free, people who get a solar power system for their house will see a cut in their electric bill. They can save a lot of money. For one thing, there are savings from using less grid power. For another, there may be additional savings because of a policy called net metering. This policy, which exists in the United States and some other areas, applies to people whose home power system is linked to the grid. It allows them to sell to the grid any electricity they make but do not use.

Such small solar power systems have another benefit

Did You Know?
Solar Efficiency

Solar energy has an advantage over other renewable energy sources. It is more efficient in terms of the power that can be produced from a given area of land. According to one estimate, solar power plants can produce about six times more power than biofuels or wind. (To produce a sizable amount of electricity using wind power, many wind turbines—which are sort of like modern windmills—must be built on a large area of land.) Solar power's advantage over water power is even greater.

Some U.S. Army tents have thin-film solar cells. They provide power for such things as laptop computers and phones.

as well. They provide a backup source of power in case of a **blackout**, or failure of the grid. They can also be good for the grid. The electricity they supply may help keep the grid from failing when the demand for electricity from the grid gets very high.

Helping the Environment

Solar energy is a clean energy source. Its use causes much less harm to the environment than do the main fuels used today. The mining of fossil fuels and uranium (used in nuclear power) requires cutting into Earth's surface. The burning of fossil fuels releases pollutants (harmful substances that damage the environment). The use of fossil fuels and nuclear fuel creates wastes and byproducts. Some of them can be very harmful, and all of them have to be disposed of in some way.

Passive solar methods for providing warmth, light, or cooling do not use any fuel at all. They do not have any noisy machinery, either. Solar cells, which turn sunshine directly into electricity, also do not make any noise. They use no mechanical generators. They do not need bulky fuel. They do not release pollutants into the air, and they do not leave wastes. Traditional power plants use huge amounts of water for cooling, but

Workers install solar panels on the roof of a house.

Did You Know?

Doing It All in One Place

A nice thing about small PV power systems is that you can put them almost anywhere. The PV panels can go on a roof or a wall or even an empty lawn. It is also possible to put many cells in one place in order to make a huge power plant. In **theory**, one plant could make all the electricity used in the United States. Such a plant would need to be located in a sunny place, such as the Southwest. It would also need to be big. How big? Experts say perhaps 87 miles (140 kilometers) by 87 miles. Probably, no one would ever build such a plant. Making and installing so many PV panels would cost a huge amount of money. So would building the long transmission lines that would be needed to carry the electricity produced to other parts of the country.

PV power stations do not. PV stations have other advantages, too. One is that PV arrays are easy to install. As a result, PV plants can be built much faster than fossil-fuel or nuclear power plants. Also, it is easier to expand PV plants as the demand for electricity rises.

In the past, people sometimes complained that PV panels placed on buildings looked ugly, but today's modern designs

27

are different. It may even be hard to notice the PV cells used on walls, roofs, or other surfaces.

Solar thermal power systems do use machinery to make electricity. Like PV power systems, though, they use no bulky fuel, and they produce virtually no pollution or wastes.

Solar Resources

The U.S. Department of Energy says that most places around the world get enough sunlight to use solar cells. Still, some parts of the world do get more sunshine than others. The North Pole and South Pole, for example, get less sunshine than regions

Some parts of the world tend to get more sunshine than other parts. Solar plants work best where there is a great deal of sunshine.

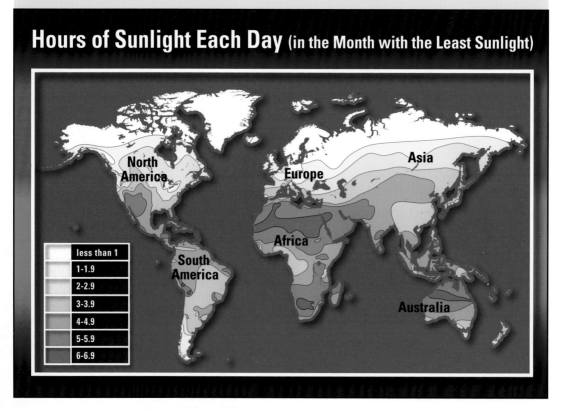

Hours of Sunlight Each Day (in the Month with the Least Sunlight)

	less than 1
	1-1.9
	2-2.9
	3-3.9
	4-4.9
	5-5.9
	6-6.9

North America
Europe
Asia
Africa
South America
Australia

closer to the **equator**. A solar power plant will work better where there is a large amount of sunshine. In the United States, the southwestern states are especially good places for building solar plants. They get a large amount of sunlight, and they have a great deal of land available. Also, there are big cities in the region that could use the power produced in the plants. Other parts of the world have similar features—a great deal of sunshine and a great deal of land. That is one reason why Spain and Portugal have a number of solar power plants. China has huge deserts that get a great deal of sunlight. In 2007, China launched a big program to build solar power plants.

Most PV cells are made from silicon, which is found in sand and many types of rock. Plenty of silicon exists. In fact, it makes up about 26 percent of Earth's crust and is the second most common substance in the crust (after oxygen). This does not mean that solar cells can be as cheap or as easy to obtain as sunshine. Silicon is usually found combined with other materials, and work must be done to separate it out. In addition, silicon is used for more things than just solar cells—computer chips, for example. So, PV cells have to share the silicon supply with other uses. Also, some PV cells are made from other materials. Still, the fact that silicon is so plentiful is one reason many people believe solar power has a bright future.

Both new and old houses can be equipped with solar panels. These panels can save homeowners a great deal of money.

CHAPTER 4

Weak Points of Solar Power

Solar energy has plenty of good points. Still, it is not perfect. The biggest drawback is that solar energy works only when the Sun shines. As a result, solar power systems do not run at night. Cost can also be a problem. Sunshine is free, but the equipment for doing something with it is not. The environment is also a concern. Solar power systems do not release pollutants, but they still may have effects on the environment.

Lack of Light

The fact that solar power systems do not work at night is a problem, but there may be reason for concern at other times, too. Solar power systems work best in bright light. During the day, however, sunlight changes all the time. In areas like the United States, a specific place generally gets more sunshine in summer than winter. Also, there is more sunshine at noon than in the early morning or late afternoon. Weather affects the amount of sunshine as well. On a cloudy or rainy day, for example, there will be little sunshine.

These facts mean that a solar power system cannot do the job all by itself. It needs help. Something must fill the gap when there is little or no sunlight. There are two basic ways to fill this gap. One is to save, or store, some energy for use when needed. The other is to have one or more additional power sources on

Solar power systems do not run as well on cloudy days, when there is little sunshine.

hand. In some cases, both approaches are used.

Batteries are a popular way of storing energy for home solar power systems. They can be charged when the Sun shines, and then, their power can be used when the Sun is gone. Some power systems store energy in the form of heat, such as in a tank of hot liquid. This heat can be used to make electricity when it gets dark. Solar thermal power systems, which work by producing heat, can easily use this method of storing energy.

Various power sources can also be used to fill the sunlight gap. If there is a link to the grid, then the grid can do the job.

Two renewable energy sources provide power for this building. There are PV cells on the roof in addition to a wind-powered turbine (at left).

In some cases, however, the grid is not available, so another backup is needed. Often, an electric generator that runs on fossil fuels serves as a backup power source. In addition, some buildings have a "hybrid" energy system that relies on two or more energy sources. An example is a wind-solar hybrid, which has one or more wind-powered electric generators plus some sort of solar power system. In this case, both sources are renewable.

Money Matters

The cost of a solar power system is increased because of the need to have another energy source or some form of energy storage for cloudy and dark days and nights. Power companies must take this into account when they plan a large solar plant. So do people who want to put a small solar power system in their house. Power companies hope that they will make enough money by selling electricity to pay the huge cost of building a power plant and linking it to the grid. Homeowners hope a new power system will cut their electric bill enough to cover the cost of building the system. In both cases, if the estimated cost is too high, then the companies and homeowners may decide not to build the new system. Some people, of course, are more interested in the environmental benefits of solar power. They

WEAK POINTS OF SOLAR POWER

may decide to get a solar power system even if it does not save them money.

In certain areas, the government may provide help that lowers the cost of solar systems. The U.S. government and some U.S. states promote the use of solar energy. They offer **tax reductions** to people who put in a solar power or heating system. The policy of net metering also helps reduce costs. It makes sure that people will be able to benefit from any extra electricity they produce.

Did You Know?
Supersized

In order to get a large amount of sunshine, a solar power plant needs to be quite big. Take, for example, the Waldpolenz Solar Park near Leipzig, Germany, which can produce 40 megawatts of electricity. The plant covers an area of about 270 acres (110 hectares). It uses thin-film solar cells and is the world's biggest thin-film PV power system, using 550,000 thin-film solar modules. A good example of a large solar thermal power plant is Nevada Solar One at Boulder City. The plant covers 400 acres (162 hectares) and has a power capacity of 64 megawatts.

Environment
Solar energy is much cleaner than the energy produced with fossil fuels. Still, the use of solar energy can affect the environment. One concern is the silicon and other materials used in solar-energy equipment. Getting these materials takes work. So does the manufacture of the equipment. Often, both types of work are powered by fossil fuels. Burning these fossil fuels releases pollutants.

Also, substances may leak into the environment during the processing of the materials. Some of these substances are poisonous. Harmful substances may also be released during the making of solar-energy equipment. Overall, however, the pollution linked to solar energy is much less than that linked to fossil fuels.

Another concern is land use. Every second, Earth receives a huge amount of solar energy, but the amount hitting any given point on Earth is small. For this reason, solar power stations have to cover big areas, so that they can collect enough energy to make useful amounts of electricity. In taking over a big area, however, they may harm the living things found there.

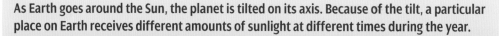
As Earth goes around the Sun, the planet is tilted on its axis. Because of the tilt, a particular place on Earth receives different amounts of sunlight at different times during the year.

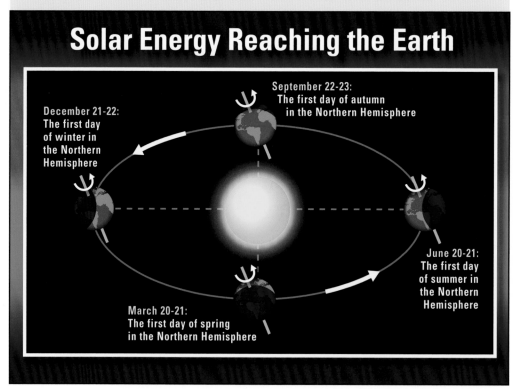

Did You Know?

Solar Cars and Planes

Using electricity to power cars is nothing new. The first electric cars, which ran on batteries, appeared more than a century ago. Could solar power be used to run cars, too? Could solar power also be used for aircraft? In order to provide enough electricity to run a car, a big solar array is needed. A good example is a little two-seat electric car called the Solartaxi. It was driven around the world in 2007 and 2008 to draw attention to solar power. For power, the Solartaxi had a trailer with 65 square feet (6 square meters) of solar cells. Future PV cells may take up less space, but the array needed to power a car will still be relatively large. Also, big batteries are needed so the car can run when there is little or no sunshine. Thus far, the only solar vehicles made have been experimental ones. This is also the case with solar planes, which need large arrays but must also be very light in weight. The wings of the solar plane shown here were covered with solar cells.

Progress, Prospects, and Dreams

Solar devices keep improving. Today's devices and systems are better than the ones that were in use a few years ago. PV cells get cheaper and cheaper, and batteries and other storage devices get better. Meanwhile, scientists keep finding new ways to use solar energy. At the same time, people are getting more and more worried about fossil fuels and their probable effects on Earth's climate.

As a result of these trends, sunshine will probably provide a larger share of the energy we use in the future. It is hard to say how fast this will happen. It is also hard to know how big this share will be. Both depend on how quickly solar technology improves. They also depend on what happens with other renewable energy sources. Their cost might go down, too. Still, solar energy seems to have a bright future.

Cost Down, Efficiency Up

PV cells are a good example of how solar technology has progressed. Cells in the 1950s did not work very well. Their efficiency was low. Efficiency measures how good a cell is at turning the light it receives into electricity. Efficiency tells how much of the received energy is converted into useful electricity. In the 1950s, the efficiency of PV cells was about 6 percent. Even with that low efficiency, the cells cost a lot of money. They

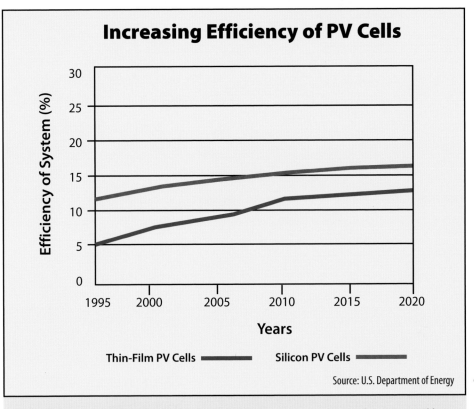

Increasing Efficiency of PV Cells

Source: U.S. Department of Energy

Thin-Film PV Cells   Silicon PV Cells

The efficiency of different types of solar cells has increased over the years and is expected to continue to do so.

cost so much that they were used mainly in spacecraft. Space was the only place where they were the cheapest power source.

Over the years, scientists came up with new and improved PV cells. Meanwhile, the prices of standard cells dropped. All this made it possible to use cells in more ways. With thin-film technology, cells could even be put on flexible surfaces such as fabric. Progress in solar cells also made it possible to build more big PV power plants. Currently, many cells have an efficiency of 15 percent or more, depending on the type of cell. Some experimental cells have much higher efficiencies.

Solar thermal power methods have also improved. In early 2008, the company Stirling Energy Systems achieved the amazingly high efficiency of 31.25 percent with one of

Solar panels on the roof provide the power for this boat, which carries passengers in London, England.

its SunCatcher solar dishes. This was a new record for a solar power system. The previous record, 29.4 percent, had stood for 24 years. The SunCatcher uses a dish reflector to concentrate the Sun's heat on a Stirling engine, which runs a generator. In comparison, many fossil-fuel power plants have an efficiency in the range of about 30 to 35 percent.

Since the efficiency of solar systems has been improving, up-to-date PV and thermal solar power plants can make electricity more cheaply than older solar plants. This may help convince developers to choose solar as an energy source when it is time to build a new power plant. Of course, the efficiency of other technologies is getting better all the time, too. Developers have hard decisions to make when they must decide which technology is the best choice for them.

Helping Other Technologies

Solar energy may help us use other promising new energy sources. Take, for example, the device known as a hydrogen **fuel cell**. A hydrogen fuel cell is a very clean energy source that makes electricity by combining hydrogen with oxygen from the air. The chief waste product is water. The electricity from these cells could be used to power a car.

Hydrogen is extremely common in nature. It is, for instance, found in water. There is a big problem, however, in getting the hydrogen: A great deal of energy has to be used to do so. The energy can be gotten by burning fossil fuels, but they release

Space Power

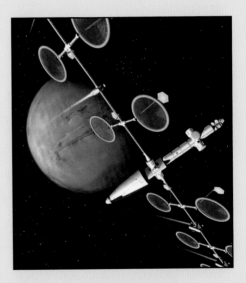

Some scientists propose putting a solar power station—such as the one shown here—in space. In space, the Sun always shines and there are no clouds. A solar power station—equipped with many solar panels in orbit around Earth—could soak up huge amounts of sunlight. The station would beam the power to the ground, perhaps using radio waves. Currently, this is all theory. Scientists do not know yet whether such a system would work. Even if it would work, scientists do not know whether it would cost too much to be practical.

These buses run on hydrogen fuel cells. Solar power is used to produce the hydrogen.

pollutants and will not last forever. Some experts think solar energy might someday supply the answer. Either electricity from PV cells or heat from a solar thermal system could supply the needed energy. Either way, by linking solar energy with the hydrogen fuel cell, scientists could combine the strong points of both technologies and avoid their drawbacks. Solar energy is not very good for powering vehicles, but the fuel cell is ideal. Solar power does not work at night, but fuel cells can work at any time of day. Fuel cells need a convenient way of producing hydrogen. Solar energy might provide it.

Looking Ahead

Currently, the most remarkable developments in solar energy involve PV cells. News stories tell of new types of PV cells and new ways of using cells. In 2008, for example, scientists at the Massachusetts Institute of Technology came up with a way to turn windows into collectors of light for solar cells. They put special dyes on the glass of a window that has PV cells at its edges. The dyes let through much of the light that hits the glass, so the window still works like a window. The dyes also send some of the light energy to the solar cells. The result is that the entire surface of the window can be used to make electricity. More work is needed on the idea, but researchers say the system would be easy to manufacture and not too expensive. It might be ready for practical use within a few years.

> ## In Their Own Words
>
> "As the technology for solar cells gets better and better, this form of clean, renewable energy will find more applications that take up less space and produce more electricity, to meet the energy needs of our homes, schools, and businesses."
>
> Former U.S. Secretary of Energy
> Samuel Bodman, 2005

Advances in PV cells are an important reason why the use of sunshine to make electric power is expected to continue to grow in coming years. The use of sunshine is also likely to grow because of improvements in solar thermal power systems. Experts, however, do not expect the growth to be huge. Because solar power does not work when there is no sunshine, a power company cannot use it to supply what is called the **base load**. That is the minimum amount of energy the company promises to supply, at any time of day. Currently, fossil fuels, nuclear power, and water power are common ways of supplying the base load. Solar power can help power companies supply electricity, however. During the day, demand for electricity tends to rise. Solar power can help power companies meet this extra demand.

The U.S. Department of Energy predicted in 2009 that by the year 2030, solar power would produce almost 0.5 percent of the grid electricity generated by renewable sources. In comparison, the department said that, in 2007, solar power provided only about 0.3 percent of the electricity from renewable sources. Overall, renewable sources—including solar power—were expected to account for about 15 percent of the electricity produced for the grid in 2030.

A solar-powered car at the North American Solar Challenge, one of many competitions held to increase interest in solar power.

Did You Know?
Solar Competitions

Contests are regularly held to increase interest in solar energy. The U.S. Energy Department runs a Solar **Decathlon** every two years. Teams of college students take part, trying to design and build the best solar-powered house. Races of solar-powered cars also get a large amount of attention. One such race, the World Solar Challenge, takes place every two years in Australia. Another race, for people from the United States and Canada, is the North American Solar Challenge. The race is also held every other year.

The U.S. Energy Department sponsors a contest especially for sixth, seventh, and eighth graders. The contest is called the Junior Solar Sprint/Hydrogen Fuel Cell Car Competition. Teams of students build and race model cars that are run by solar power or hydrogen fuel cells.

A solar-powered house at the Solar Decathlon.

GLOSSARY

AC: Alternating current, a type of electric current, or flow of electricity, that reverses its direction many times a second.

active method: A method for using solar energy that involves the use of electricity or machines—for example, a solar heating system that uses a pump.

base load: The demand for power placed on an electrical power supply system.

biofuels: Renewable fuels that come from living things.

blackout: A total loss of electric power supply from the power grid; also known as a power outage.

climate: The weather and overall environmental conditions in a place as measured over a long period of time.

concentrator: A device used to collect a great deal of sunlight over a large area so the combined energy can be used in a smaller area. Concentrators often use lenses or mirrors.

DC: Direct current, a type of electric current, or flow of electricity, that always goes in the same direction.

decathlon: In sports, a competition that involves 10 different athletic events.

device: Something that does some action.

equator: An imaginary circle around the middle of Earth, halfway between the North and South Poles.

fossil fuel: A fuel, such as coal, natural gas, or oil, that was formed underground over millions of years from the remains of prehistoric plants and animals. Such fuels are not renewable.

fuel cell: A device that uses a reaction between two substances, such as hydrogen and oxygen, to make electricity.

fusion: An energy-producing process that occurs in the Sun. It involves the combination, or fusion, of atoms.

generator: A machine that is used to convert energy, such as that provided by burning fuel or by wind or water, into electricity.

grid: The general electric power system.

megawatt: A million watts.

passive method: A method for using solar energy without the help of electricity or machines—for example, a solar heating system that relies on the natural tendency of hot air or hot water to rise.

patent: For an invention, a document giving its holder the right to make and sell the invention and preventing others from making and selling the invention without the holder's permission.

photovoltaic: Referring to the action of solar cells and panels that make electricity from sunlight; photovoltaic cells collect sunlight and convert it into electricity.

power: The rate at which energy is used to do work. People often say "electric power" or "power" to refer to electricity; for example, *solar power* commonly means electricity produced from solar energy.

power plant: A place for the production of electric power, also sometimes called a "power station."

PV: Photovoltaic.

radiation: Various kinds of energy given off by objects; examples include light and the harmful rays and particles given off by "radioactive" materials.

radioactive waste: Materials that give off harmful radiation, or radioactivity, and are left over from the production of nuclear power.

renewable: A resource that never gets used up. Energy sources such as sunlight and wind are renewable; sources such as coal, natural gas, and oil are nonrenewable.

reservoir: A large body of water created by people, often behind a dam.

semiconductor: A substance that conducts electricity, but not as well as a metal.

solar array: A group of solar modules that are linked together.

solar cell: A small device that makes electricity from sunlight.

solar module: A group of solar cells that are linked together.

solar panel: Another name for a solar module or solar array.

tax reduction: A decrease in taxes that someone must pay.

terrorist: A person who uses violence for political purposes.

theory: A statement or idea that explains why something happens.

tides: The rise and fall of the oceans twice each day, caused by the gravity of the Sun and the Moon.

transistor: A small electronic device, consisting of a semiconductor and other parts, that controls the flow of electric current in computers, radios, television sets, and other machines.

turbine: A machine that produces a turning action, which can be used to make electricity. The turning action may be caused by steam, wind, or some other energy source.

versatile: Useful in different ways.

watt: A common unit of measurement for the rate at which electric energy is used.

Read these books:

Fridell, Ron. *Earth-Friendly Energy*. Minneapolis: Lerner, 2009.

Kodis, Michelle. *Turn Me On: 100 Easy Ways to Use Solar Energy*. Layton, Utah: Gibbs Smith, 2009.

Povey, Karen D. *Energy Alternatives*. San Diego: Lucent, 2007.

Tabak, John. *Solar and Geothermal Energy*. New York: Facts On File, 2009.

Thomas, Isabel. *The Pros and Cons of Solar Power*. New York: Rosen, 2007.

Look up these Web sites:

Department of Energy, National Renewable Energy Laboratory
http://www.nrel.gov/learning/sr_solar.html

How Solar Cells Work
http://www.howstuffworks.com/solar-cell.htm

NASA: The Edge of Sunshine
http://science.nasa.gov/headlines/y2002/08jan_sunshine.htm

TreeHugger: How Does Solar Energy Work?
http://www.treehugger.com/files/2008/03/how-solar-energy-works.php

Key Internet search terms:

photovoltaic, renewable, solar energy, solar power, Sun

INDEX

The abbreviation *ill.* stands for illustration, and *ills.* stands for illustrations. Page references to illustrations and maps are in *italic* type.

About the Author

Richard Hantula has written, edited, and translated books and articles on science and technology for more than three decades. He was the senior U.S. editor for the *Macmillan Encyclopedia of Science*.